This is

Soccer

Published by **Gollancz/Witherby**
in association with ***When Saturday Comes***

Compiled and Edited by
Doug Cheeseman
Mike Alway
Andy Lyons
Philip Cornwall

Principal Photographers
Peter Robinson
Tom Jenkins
Tony Davis
Alistair Berg

Foreword by
Patrick Barclay

This is

Images of World Cup USA '94

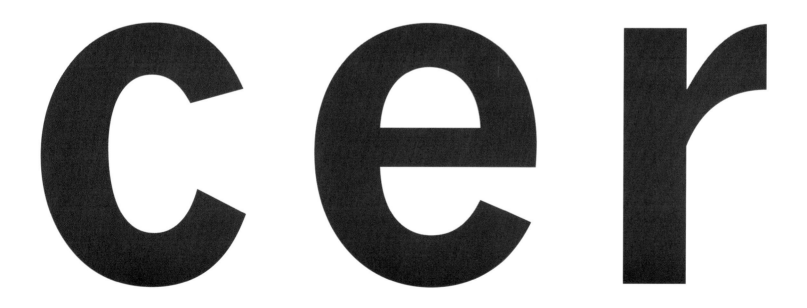

This is **Soccer**

This is Soccer was researched and compiled with a particular approach to picture selection in mind. We have not attempted to tell the story of USA '94, already familiar from the thousands of action pictures published during and since the tournament. Instead, the photographs chosen are those that capture the spirit of the World Cup, where events taking place off the pitch are at least as important as anything that happens on it. So, no goalmouth mêlées, or infernal 'samba' parties, but instead a behind-the-scenes study of Gheorghe Hagi's calf muscles and Irish fans' dehydrated euphoria in Giants stadium.

In short, just a glimpse of what it was like to be on the touchline, in the stadia or just in the country during World Cup USA '94. Write your name in the left-hand corner and claim it's an album of your own holiday snaps. No one will suspect.

This is **Soccer**, Editors

Foreword

By **Patrick Barclay**, *Observer* football correspondent

The 1994 World Cup was not so very different, in terms of atmosphere, from others I have experienced. The main change was that the stadia were usually full – as they damn well should be for the biggest event in this game or any other. Glory be! FIFA got it right. The sceptics were routed.

More than once during football's blazing summer of delightful self-discovery, when creative players received some relief from lunging studs and Pavlovian linesmanship, the thought occurred that America, or more precisely the part of it known as the United States, might be worth considering as a permanent home for the World Cup. There were irritants: the automatons who frequently appeared behind hotel and airline desks in the guise of human beings there to help; the massive security presence surrounding some matches, which made you wonder if someone had forgotten to inform the organizers that neither Iraq nor England had qualified; the occasional discovery that all bars in the neighbourhood where you happened to be were showing basketball or something other than a World Cup match; and, of course, the bewildering desire to ⟶

5

continued

engage you in conversation about O.J. Simpson. But these were minor. The World Cup fitted the United States like fingers in a snug glove.

It was welcomed by a polyglot society. The fact that the majority of the population cared little or nothing for it was irrelevant, for within their midst was a genuine football community made up of at least as many people as an entire, substantial European nation, such as Spain. I have been to a World Cup in Spain. I have been to one in Mexico, and one in Italy, and in each case the pattern was the same: hardcore local interest was chauvinistic, expiring with the host team's demise. The atmosphere relied more on visitors, fermenting wonderfully when they mingled as did – to mention but one occasion of cherished memory – the Brazilians and Scots in Seville in 1982. For me that sort of thing is the heart of the World Cup, and how strongly it beat in 1994. Orlando is never likely to forget the carnival weekend when the Irish, Dutch, Belgians and Mexicans jammed its little downtown pleasure zone, singing and dancing while battalions of police officers stood around, some bored, others grinning as the infection spread, but all, in effect, relieved of their duties on full pay.

The World Cup adapted to its siting in a country unfamiliar with international football culture by being on its best behaviour. Alan Rothenberg, the Californian lawyer who led the USA '94 organization, called it a 'love-in', and self-conscious elements of that are addressed in the photograph on page 11 of this book. The Americans were ready for the worst, too, but page 39 emphasizes that the scene around the stadia often resembled a jobless rally for the nation's bouncers. Those of us who had come from England were bound to reflect on how things might have turned out had Messrs Overmars, Bergkamp and Koeman, not to mention referee Assenmacher, been kinder to Graham Taylor's regime in the qualifying stages. Who can say? I for one was happy to settle for five weeks' relief from anxiety. It has become something of a cliché, I know, to praise Ireland's supporters, but from their sun-scorched faces radiated a respectful fervour that had much to do with the seduction of borderline Americans in the media and elsewhere. The Irish numbers were staggering and when they took over Giants Stadium for what Italy's most prominent sports newspaper dubbed the Brooklyn-Queens derby, the bandwagon of interest accelerated; the US team, starting their campaign in Michigan the same weekend, can have felt no more at home.

Soccer was big-time for those few weeks. No one should doubt that. It was no love-in, though, for American reporters. Just as some visitors were shocked by the semi-official conspiracy that jacked up rates for hotel rooms – a reminder that we were in the land of opportunity – the local media were taken aback by FIFA's apparent policy of access-starvation. Yet coverage in the American papers compared favourably on matters of detail – if not always style and perception – with that sent out from home. The message was received, and transmitted, that this game of soccer really mattered to people. The extent to which it can mirror the condition of a nation was to be illustrated in the most distressing way when Andrés Escobar, the Colombian defender, was shot dead after defeat at the hosts' hands had confirmed his team's suspiciously early return. All America was stunned then. But also there was a fascination with the trivial aspects of real foreigners, as opposed to ethnic groups; some articles dwelt on the phe-

nomenon of sports stars with long hair. The Argentine trio on page 63 may look routine to us – we know their nation is inspired by Paul Walsh – but to the average American they were wacky guys.

I was not terribly bothered, to tell you the truth, what the average American thought, because I had never been under the slightest illusion that to them the World Cup was anything else but a passing parade. I was more interested in the football community, who were either hungry for information or were full of it. I liked their sense of proportion about the home team's advance through workrate and tactical discipline, their appreciation of more gifted participants. They would not have endorsed Rothenberg's aberrant remark about the banishment of Maradona being 'an asterisk footnote'. Before the tournament Maradona had said that, whatever fate had in store for Argentina, 'I'll be sure I gave everything'. In the event, according to FIFA's medical officer, he *took* just about everything. Is that fatalism in his eyes on pages 46–7? Turn from there to the Irishmen on pages 26–7, feel your heart leap, and relive a summer of overwhelmingly pleasant surprise. □

Language Barriers

When visiting a
new country, make
an effort to learn
the language...

Love at First Sight

Alan Rothenberg,
Chairman of World
Cup USA 1994,
Inc., described the
event as 'a love-in',
and sent a plane
up above the Rose
Bowl to prove
the point.
The Romanian
players take it all
in their stride

South Korean fans
in Boston. Their
team were
eliminated in the
First Round, after
drawing twice and
then unluckily
losing 3–2
to Germany

Where questions
were answered.
The World Cup
Information
Centre outside the
Pasadena
Rose Bowl

Swedish striker
Martin Dahlin
recovers after
being substituted
during the
Quarter-Final win
over Romania

The Gentle Touch

Romania's
Gheorghe Hagi
finds an innovative
way to cool down

Belgian players
line up before
their Second-
Round game with
Germany. The
referee, Kurt
Röthlisberger of
Switzerland, was
sent home by FIFA
shortly afterwards,
for failing to
award them a
clear penalty.
Belgium lost 3–2

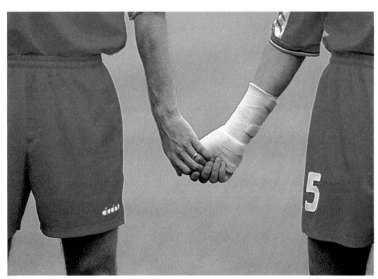

Two fans arrive early
at the Cotton Bowl in
Dallas for Germany v
South Korea. The
tournament broke
attendance records,
but most of the sta-
diums didn't fill up
until after the games
kicked off. 'Scalpers'
were frequently sell-
ing tickets outside
venues

One of the few occasions that a match finished after dusk. Dutch fans stay late at RFK Stadium in Washington to celebrate their team's unimpressive 2–1 win over Saudi Arabia

Italian coach Arrigo Sacchi manages a smile at the press conference after Italy's First-Round defeat by Ireland. The journalists were considerably less cheerful. 'Betrayal,' said *Corriere dello Sport*, adding, 'Sacchi has gone bonkers'

Sacchi's Brazilian
counterpart,
Carlos Alberto
Parreira, looks
glum the day
before Brazil's
Semi-Final with
Sweden. The
Brazilian fans
cheered the
players' names
as they were
announced before
each game, but
Parreira's was
always booed

Building Sights

Fans descend
the spiral
staircase outside
Giants Stadium,
New York/New Jersey

The view from
behind the goal at
Giants Stadium.
Not recommended
for vertigo
sufferers

Personal Growth

Xavier Azkargorta,
Bolivia's Basque
coach. A qualified
eye surgeon and
the cultivator of an
extraordinary
moustache

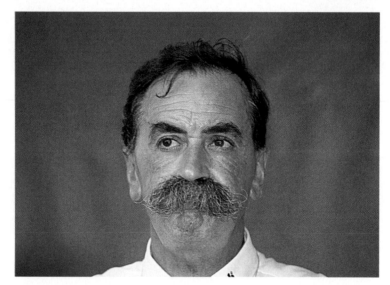

The unmistakable
Carlos Valderrama,
captain of
Colombia. His
team were
the biggest
disappointment of
the World Cup,
eliminated in the
First Round having
lost two of their
three matches

Euphoria

The ball's in the Italian net and Ireland's World Cup is off to a flying start. It was the game's only goal

I'm a Believer

Romania's coach Anghel Iordanescu holds up a crucifix. He kissed his good luck charm, a book of Romanian saints, every time the team scored

A Saudi
photographer
prays to Mecca
during half-time
in the match
with Holland

Sound and Vision

A TV technician
homes in on a
conversation;
Sweden's Roland
Nilsson stays
focused on the
job at hand

Paying Respects

Soldier Field,
Chicago, observes
a minute's silence
for Colombian
defender Andrés
Escobar, who was
shot dead shortly
after his return
home. The killing
appears to have
been motivated by
the own goal
Escobar scored
during Colombia's
2–1 defeat by
the USA

Samson Siasia of
Nigeria, before
their First-Round
match with
Greece

A German fan
dozing in the
shade, Dallas;
Jürgen Klinsmann
watches the final
minutes of
Germany's
Second-Round
match with
Belgium after
being substituted

They Came From Outer Space

A large number of
overseas fans
came to the USA
on trips sponsored
by corporate
employers, such
as these Dutch
fans wearing the
company colours

One of the World Cup motifs follows the instructions of a Washington traffic sign

Underemployed LA stewards take the weight off their feet

The distinctive red
footwear of
Belgian midfielder
Enzo Scifo;
anonymous
Bulgarian legs
shielding the ball
prior to the
Quarter-Final
with Germany

Under the
antiquated stands
of the Stanford
Stadium, San
Francisco, for
Brazil v Cameroon

Exits and Entrances

A fan seeks
relief from the
scorching heat of
the Citrus Bowl,
Orlando

Jack Charlton
takes the
straightforward
approach to a
training-ground
penalty

Roberto Baggio
practises free-
kicks against a flat
defence before the
Semi-Final with
Bulgaria in which
he scored both
Italy's goals

Altered Image

Argentina's Diego
Maradona at a
press conference
after the
announcement
that he had
tested positive
for a banned
substance. Before
the tournament he
said, 'I am trying
to force that extra
few per cent out.
God willing, we
will return as
World Champions.
If not, I'll be sure I
gave everything'

Twelve-foot people walk the earth and shiny silver objects appear in the sky. The fifteenth World Cup is underway

The De Boers,
Ronald and Frank
(or Frank and
Ronald?), wait in
the tunnel before
their Second-
Round victory
over the Irish;
Jorge Rodriguez
and Claudio
Suarez of Mexico
take in the
surroundings
prior to their First-
Round victory,
also against the
Republic of Ireland

USA 1,
Switzerland 1,
attracting a few
customers at
Michael Jordan's
restaurant in
Chicago

US defender Alexi Lalas plays guitar in a rock band. Tracks on his first CD, released just before the Finals, include 'Kickin' Balls' and 'Wait Up For Me'. 'Music and soccer are the perfect match,' Lalas says. 'Precision, timing and understanding are key ingredients to doing each well'

NYPD Blue

The police come
under fire during
Bulgaria's Second-
Round victory
over Mexico

A referee clutches
the ball. On his
left hand, the
official World
Cup watch,
which runs in
forty-five-minute
cycles

Precious Time

Substitute John Aldridge lets FIFA's touchline official know how long he has been waiting to be allowed on to the pitch during Ireland's match with Mexico. Aldridge was later fined $1,850 for his outburst – but scored a crucial goal

The owner of a sponsor's pink rabbit costume takes a breather

'You cause a commotion, I'll shove it under my jacket and sneak out the back way.' FIFA's President, João Havelange, and General Secretary, Sepp Blatter, huddle round the World Cup trophy

USA fans aboard
the Soccer Train
from Boston to the
Foxboro Stadium
look forward to
South Korea v
Bolivia

Argentinians keep
the faith prior to
their First-Round
defeat by
Bulgaria, the day
after Diego
Maradona had
failed a drugs test

Without Maradona for
the first time in a
World Cup game since
1978, Argentina's
Redondo, Rodriguez
and Batistuta prepare
to take a free-kick

A Brazilian fan
takes to the skies
during the Final

The Middle of Nowhere

'Dear Mum, Have
arrived safely...'
A supporter from
Tipperary at
Newark Airport,
New Jersey

Nonchalant Italian substitutes collect their thoughts while their team-mates edge past Spain, 2–1, in the Quarter-Finals

Bulgarian reserves
viewed through
the glass dugout
during the match
with Mexico

Object Lessons

Irish supporters
sun-worshipping
at Giants Stadium
before the Ireland
v Italy match

An inquisitive fan
inspects the XV
sign displayed at
all the venues to
show this was the
fifteenth World Cup

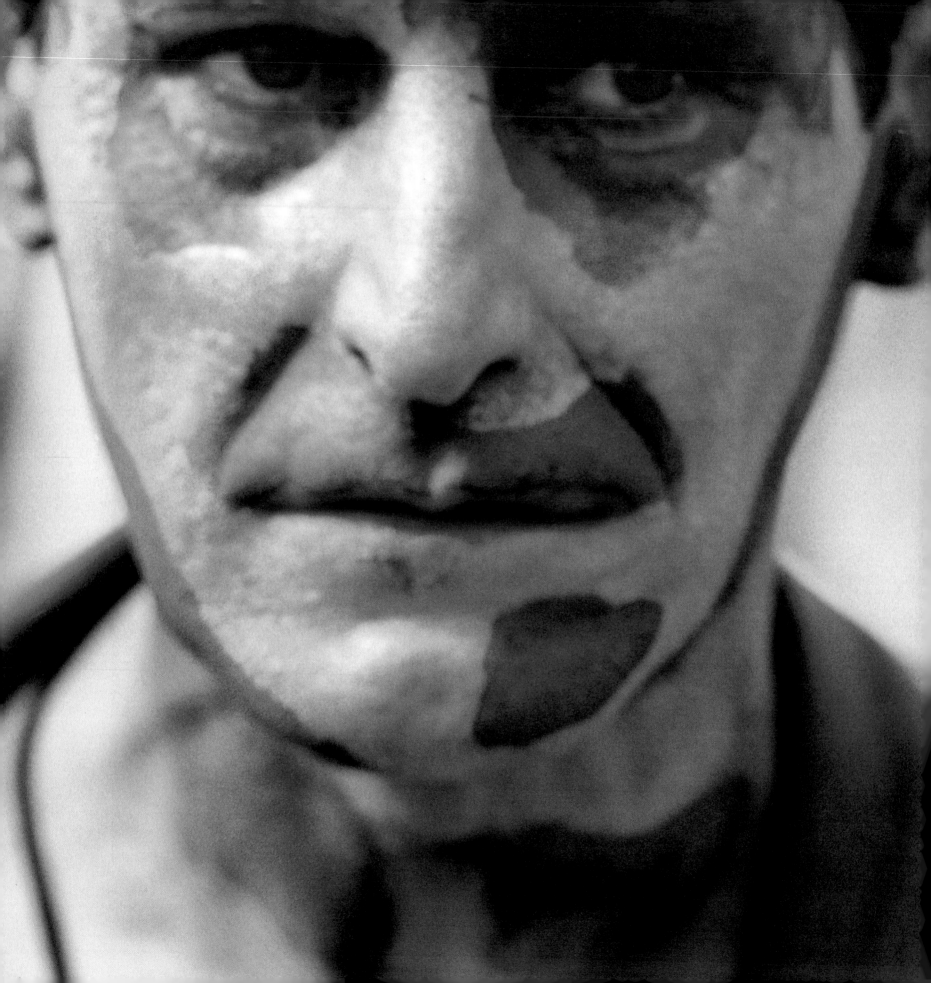

A Brazilian fan
makes a strong
impression with
face paint

Lost Cause

Bulgaria 2

Germany 1

German coach Berti Vogts's mirror image at a news conference following the Quarter-Final defeat by Bulgaria. 'The only mistake made was deciding against [reserve goalkeeper] Andreas Köpke,' Vogts said. 'I put my trust in Bodo Illgner's experience and was disappointed'

Food and Drink

Argentinian fans in
Dunkin' Donuts,
cutting up
papelitos, the
confetti made from
newspapers which
is thrown when
their team walks
on to the pitch

Emil Kostadinov of
Bulgaria in need
of refreshment

If the Cap Fits

A solitary Mexico 1994 cap (look closely, bottom row above the vest) is the only World Cup souvenir on display at a street stall in New York

A fan in California finds a use for more traditional headgear

Mr Torres
Cadena,
Colombia's
representative in
the latter stages
of the Finals,
chases an errant
inflatable during
the Bulgaria v
Germany
Quarter-Final

Different Ball Game

A soccer convert,
with radio tuned
to the half-time
scores?

Tab Ramos hovers
over a Californian
liquor store; flags
and bunting
brighten up a
Manhattan
office block

Liquid Assets

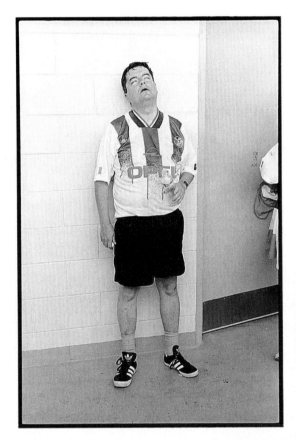

'They can drink anything they like – water, beer, champagne – just so long as they are on the touchline.' FIFA Press Officer Guido Tognoni laying down the conditions under which players were permitted to take drinks during matches

The heat posed problems for the supporters, too, as this dehydrated Ireland fan at the Citrus Bowl discovered

In the drink.
A cool Paul McGrath
meets the press

Christos
Karkamanis is
beaten in training.
He was the most
successful of the
three goalkeepers
used by Greece.
He let in only two
goals; compatriots
Minou and
Atmatzidis
conceded
four each

Cameroon defender Thomas Libiih retrieves the ball after one of the six Russian goals in the countries' First-Round match

Automobile Association

Mexican shoppers
dodge the traffic
in downtown
New York;
on the West
coast, cars
shoot past a
freeway mural
en route to
Los Angeles airport

Raí de Souza Oliveira, known by his first name. 'Raí is an idol. There is no other player like him,' said Brazil's coach, Carlos Parreira, before the tournament. He was left out of the team for the Final

Franco Baresi
steps up to collect
his runners-up
medal from UEFA
President Lennart
Johansson,
avoiding eye
contact with the
World Cup trophy.
He had missed
Italy's first penalty
in the shoot-out

A Dutch fan gets to
the point

This is **Soccer**
Images of World Cup USA '94

First published in Great Britain 1994
by Gollancz/Witherby
A Division of the Cassell group
Villiers House, 41/47 Strand,
London WC2N 5JE

© *When Saturday Comes* and
Gollancz/Witherby 1994
Foreword © Patrick Barclay 1994

A catalogue record for this book is available from the British Library.

ISBN 0 575 05892 7

Typesetting and picture origination by Fastpoint Ltd, 4-8 Pear Tree Street, London EC1V 3SB. Tel: 0171 454 7801

Printed and bound in Spain by
Cronion S.A., Barcelona.

This is **Soccer**
Photographers

The first five photographers listed were commissioned to work on **This is Soccer,** and the photographs used are published here for the first time.

Peter Robinson

Is Director of Photography for FIFA and has been a specialist football photographer for thirty years, first covering the World Cup in 1970. He also contributed to *Shot! A Photographic Record of Football in the Seventies* published in the spring of 1994. He is now taking a break from photography to take a course in Interactive Multi-Media Studies at the Royal College of Art, by the end of which he hopes to be able to explain exactly what that means.

3, 4, 10–11, 15, 16, 28, 30–31, 32–3, 34–5, 40, 54–5, 56, 56–7, 59, 66–7, 67, 74–5, 78, 82, 88–9, 90–91, 94

Tom Jenkins

Went to USA '94 for the *Guardian* and the *Observer*. He covers a range of sports, from bowling to boxing, for the *Guardian*. He photographed the 1992 World Cup (the cricket version) in Australasia and has even dabbled in fashion photography. A Crystal Palace fan, he played in the same junior side as John Salako. Or so he claims.

8, 8, 8, 9, 20–21, 23, 40–41, 48, 50–51, 51, 70–71, 72, 72

Tony Davis

Is a freelance photographer specializing in football. He covered the 1990 World Cup, the last European Championships

and the 1994 African Nations Cup in Tunisia. His work regularly appears in *When Saturday Comes,* and he is currently working on the updated version of *The Football Grounds of Great Britain* by Simon Inglis.

12–13, 13, 18–19, 22, 53, 58, 60–61, 74, 92

Alistair Berg

Is a freelance photographer with Gamma Agency. He has produced work on the African Nations Cup, the Brazilian League and the last two World Cups. His work regularly appears in *When Saturday Comes.* He had his light meter stolen somewhere in the Dallas Cotton Bowl and would be delighted to hear from anyone who knows the person responsible.

18, 34, 36–7, 38–9, 42–3, 78–9, 86

Piers Allardyce

Is a freelance photographer working for, amongst others, *Melody Maker, Q, When Saturday Comes* and Tottenham fanzine *Cock-a-Doodle-Doo.*

39, 77, 80

The other photographs came from the sources listed below. Where two names are given the first is the copyright holder, the second is the photographer.

Dave Modell

Was commissioned by the *Independent* magazine and *New York Times* magazine to follow the contingent of Irish fans. He is a freelance photojournalist.

26–7, 64, 68–9, 82

Mark Leech

Is a freelance football photographer who has covered three of the last four World cups. He works regularly for titles such as *France Football* and *90 Minutes.*

17, 25, 43, 84–5

Tim Hunt	**65, 68, 76**
Inpho – Billy Stickland	**44, 48–9, 89**
Inpho – James Meehan	**83**
Allsport – Simon Bruty	**33**
Allsport – Chris Cole	**63**
Bob Thomas – Jerome Prevost	**62**
Bob Thomas – Bob Thomas	**24**
Reuter/Hulton – Andre Camara	**21**
Reuter/Hulton – Yannis Behrakis	**45**
Reuter/Hulton – em-Channel 13*	**46–47**
Reuter/Hulton – Michael Urban	**73**
Reuter/Hulton – Yannis Behrakis	**84**
Reuter/Hulton – Sam Mircovich	**86–87**
Colorsport – Andrew Cowie	**30**
Grant Fleming	**80–81**
Gary Leonard	**14**
Photonews – Tim de Waele	**29**
Press Association – Gerard Julien	**52**

*Argentinian TV station

Photos are listed alphabetically
by description. The key word
(in bold) being either nationality,
venue or particular detail

Photo Index

Description	Page	Source
Argentina's Redondo, Rodriguez and Batistuta	63	Allsport
Argentinian fans in Dunkin' Donuts	74	Tony Davis
Argentinian fans stay loyal to Maradona	62	Bob Thomas
Belgian players hold hands	17	Mark Leech
Belgium's Enzo Scifo's red boots	40	Peter Robinson
Bolivia's coach, Xavier Azkargorta	24	Bob Thomas
Brazil hold the trophy aloft	89	Inpho
Brazil's Carlos Parreira before the Semi-Final	21	Reuter/Hulton
Brazil's Raí viewed from behind	88–9	Peter Robinson
Brazilian fan takes to the skies	65	Tim Hunt
Brazilian fan with painted face	70–71	Tom Jenkins
Bulgaria v Germany, one ball in the net	72	Tom Jenkins
Bulgaria v Germany, two balls in the net	72	Tom Jenkins
Bulgarian player shields the ball	40–41	Tom Jenkins
Bulgarian substitutes from behind dugout	67	Peter Robinson
Cameroon's Libiih retrieves the ball, again	84–5	Mark Leech
Coke advert and Emil Kostadinov injured	74–5	Peter Robinson
Colombia's Andrés Escobar commemorated	32–3	Peter Robinson
Colombia's Carlos Valderrama	25	Mark Leech
Chicago – large inflatable ball	3	Peter Robinson
Fan next to World Cup 'XV' sign	68	Tim Hunt
Fan passes stewards and heads for the shade	42–3	Alistair Berg
Fan with 'This Is Soccer, Sucker' board	92	Tony Davis
Fans arrive early for game	18	Alistair Berg
FIFA's Havelange and Blatter with the trophy	59	Peter Robinson
German coach Berti Vogts reflects on defeat	73	Reuter/Hulton
German fan snoozing	34	Alistair Berg
Germany's Jürgen Klinsmann watching game	34–5	Peter Robinson
Greek goalkeeper Karkamanis in training	84	Reuter/Hulton
Holland fans celebrate in empty stadium	18–19	Tony Davis
Holland fans in orange suits	36–7	Alistair Berg
Holland's Ronald & Frank de Boer	50–51	Tom Jenkins
Ireland's John Aldridge argues with FIFA official	56–7	Peter Robinson
Ireland's manager, Jack Charlton, in training	44	Inpho
Ireland's Paul McGrath meets the press	83	Inpho
Irish fan arrives alone in coach station	64	Dave Modell
Irish fans resting outside Giants Stadium	68–9	Dave Modell
Irish fan suffers from dehydration	82	Dave Modell
Irish fans celebrate scoring v Italy	26–7	Dave Modell
Italian coach Sacchi cheerful after defeat	20–21	Tom Jenkins
Italian substitutes watch team-mates play Spain	66–7	Peter Robinson
Italy's Franco Baresi receives his loser's medal	90–91	Peter Robinson
Italy's Roberto Baggio practises free-kicks	45	Reuter/Hulton
Los Angeles – freeway mural	86–7	Reuter/Hulton
Maradona on video screen during drugs scandal	46–7	Reuter/Hulton
Mexican cap on sale in New York	76	Tim Hunt
Mexican fan in traditional headgear	77	Piers Allardyce
Mexican shoppers in New York	86	Alistair Berg
Mexico's Rodriguez and Suarez against Ireland	51	Tom Jenkins
Moon and floodlights in the sky	48–9	Inpho
New York – Giants Stadium inside view	23	Tom Jenkins
New York – Giants Stadium's spiral staircase	22	Tony Davis
New York – High rise flags in Manhattan	80–81	Grant Fleming
New York – Sponsor's rabbit has a rest	58	Tony Davis
Nigeria's Samson Siasia with hand on heart	33	Allsport
Opening ceremony – twelve-foot people	48	Tom Jenkins
Photographers index photo	94	Peter Robinson
Police dodge ball on touchline	54–5	Peter Robinson
Police on duty in Orlando	78–9	Alistair Berg
Police watch Donadoni take a corner	4	Peter Robinson
Referee chases a large beach ball	78	Peter Robinson
Referee with World Cup watch clutches the ball	56	Peter Robinson
Romania's Gheorghe Hagi cools down	16	Peter Robinson
Romania's manager, Iordanescu, holding crucifix	28	Peter Robinson
Romanians watch love heart drawn in the sky	10–11	Peter Robinson
San Francisco – Stanford Stadium's tunnel	43	Mark Leech
Saudi photographer praying to Mecca	29	Photonews
South Korean fans in Boston (black and white)	12–13	Tony Davis
South Korean fans in Boston (colour)	13	Tony Davis
Stewards put their feet up	39	Piers Allardyce
Sweden's Martin Dahlin recovering v Romania	15	Peter Robinson
Sweden's Roland Nilsson focused	30–31	Peter Robinson
Sound technician at work	30	Colorsport
USA fans aboard the Soccer Train	60–61	Tony Davis
USA v Switzerland in Michael Jordan's bar	52	Press Association
USA's Alexi Lalas on advertising hoarding	53	Tony Davis
USA's Tab Ramos on advertising board	80	Piers Allardyce
Water bag at side of the pitch	82	Peter Robinson
World Cup information point	14	Gary Leonard
World Cup goalkeeper motif in Washington	38–9	Alistair Berg
World Cup motif reading 'Football'	8	Tom Jenkins
World Cup motif reading 'Fussball'	8	Tom Jenkins
World Cup motif reading 'Futbol'	8	Tom Jenkins
World Cup motif reading 'Soccer'	9	Tom Jenkins

Acknowledgements

**Thanks to all the following for
their contribution to this book:**
Peter Robinson, Alistair Berg,
Patrick Barclay, Tony Davis, Piers
Allardyce, Tom Jenkins, Mark
Leech, Tim Bradford, Dave
Modell, Tim Hunt, Andrew Cowie
at Colorsport, Billy Stickland at
Inpho, Monte Fresco at Bob
Thomas, Photonews in Belgium,
Grant Fleming, Gary Leonard,
Cynthia Greer, Lance Bellers,
Tony Ageh, Eamonn McCabe,
Les Jones, Steve Rapport, Dacre
Trevor-Roper at Reuter/Hulton,
Jim Dow, Jon Westbrook, Jamie
Rainbow, Action Images, Empics,
Allsport, Press Association,
Associated Press, Tim Maddox,
Paul Tarrington and Clive Truby
at Fastpoint, Ian Preece at
Gollancz and Steve Bradley at
Downtown Darkrooms

Shot!

*A Photographic Record of Football
in the Seventies*

Shot! was compiled and edited
by *When Saturday Comes*, and
published in association with
Gollancz/Witherby. The book is
both a definitive pictorial account
of a fondly remembered era and
a permanent record of the football photographer's art. Foreword
by Eamonn McCabe.

Available in good bookshops
or by mail order for **£14.49**
(including postage and packing).
Send cheques or POs payable to
When Saturday Comes to: *When
Saturday Comes*, 4th Floor, 2 Pear
Tree Court, London EC1R 0DS

When Saturday Comes

This is Soccer was compiled and
edited by *When Saturday Comes*, a
monthly independent football
magazine. *WSC* aims to cover a
wide variety of issues connected
with football culture from international match-fixing scandals to
Jürgen Klinsmann's favourite
London tourist attractions.
(Laughter, tears and everything in
between.)

The magazine is available in
most newsagents, or at the
following annual subscription
rates: **£15** (postage and packing
free) in the UK, **£20** (including
postage and packing) in the rest
of Europe and **£25** (including
postage and packing) anywhere
else in the world.

Send cheques or POs payable
to *When Saturday Comes* to: *When
Saturday Comes*, 4th Floor, 2 Pear
Tree Court, London EC1R 0DS